# POWERHOUSE POINTERS

# POWERHOUSE POINTERS

*Motivational Messages for Personal
and Professional Empowerment*

## Feona Sharhran Huff
Founder & CEO of Powerhouse Media Group

**POWERHOUSE POINTERS**
**Motivational Messages for Personal and**
**Professional Empowerment**

iUniverse books may be ordered through booksellers or by contacting:

iUniverse
1663 Liberty Drive
Bloomington, IN 47403
www.iuniverse.com
1-800-Authors (1-800-288-4677)

ISBN: 978-1-4759-4300-9 (sc)
ISBN: 978-1-4759-4301-6 (e)

Printed in the United States of America

iUniverse rev. date: 12/12/2014

1627 Weber Avenue, Suite 3
Chesapeake, VA 23325

powerhouse4ever@gmail.com
www.stepintoyourpower.net

This book is dedicated in memory of my beloved grandmother, Clara Lewis Bond Anderson — a devoted wife, mother, grandmother, great-grandmother, nurse, educator, leader and woman after God's own heart. I love and miss you Ma. You taught me how to be a powerhouse from my toddler days up until the time you left to live in heaven. You were mighty, poised, strong, courageous, determined and no nonsense. I am because you were. Lady Clara and Sir Isaac are a reflection of you and carry your name. We hold you heavily in our hearts, minds and actions.

Love, your special granddaughter,

Feona Sharhran Huff aka Fee

# Rave Reviews About Feona Sharhran Huff

"Focused and determined on her journey, Feona Sharhran Huff is indeed a POWERHOUSE example of what a focused energy can yield as a Successful Single Mom, Phenomenal Female Entrepreneur and Astounding Author! It has been my extreme pleasure to know and work with POWERHOUSE Feona Sharhran Huff." ~ *Stacie N.C. Grant, President & CEO of CG Enterprises*

I'm so happy for you. You are doing extraordinary work and your light is shining brighter everyday. ~ *Bonique Harris, President of Meet Bonique*

"Feona Sharhran Huff is a powerhouse of empowerment. As a dynamic workshop facilitator and founder of Solo Mommy Magazine, she is on the front lines teaching women how to step into their purpose and power as well as raise terrific kids.

She is a much needed voice in the area of personal power and solo parenting." ~ *Cassandra Mack, CEO of Strategies for Empowered Living, LLC*

"Feona Sharhran Huff is fueled with deep commitment, passion and expertise when it comes to providing the tools and insights for parents to reach their full potential. Our communities, families and children are challenged on so many fronts, Feona's information and inspiration offers clear cut strategies for success." ~ *Shawn Dove, Campaign Manager of Campaign for Black Male Achievement at Open Society Foundations*

"Feona Sharhran Huff makes a difference wherever she is. Her message will bring the best out of you." ~ *Ryan "Jenks" Jenkins, CEO of Poetic Soul Inc.*

# FOREWORD

When I was asked to write the foreword for "POWERHOUSE POINTERS: Motivational Messages for Personal and Professional Empowerment" by Feona Sharhran Huff, I was truly honored. However, I was also a bit nervous. I asked myself what can I write that will effectively do justice to this great literary work.

When I met Feona in 2011, it was clear from our first encounter that this woman was living on purpose! In a time when many are satisfied with quick fixes and microwave living, here was a woman who was willing to stand by her words to empower others to reach their full potential.

I had the idea of writing several books based on my experiences, knowledge and training. But having failed in the past, Feona was one of the few to encourage and support my vision and my message. She selflessly put her name on the line and invested time into sharing valuable, empowering and uplifting information with me in order to help me get my project to the next level.

My next experience with this "Powerhouse" came when I launched my wellness living blog. I had been toying with the idea but a little hesitant to step out and get it done. Feona warned me not to allow what I considered to be limitations to stop me from moving forward with an endeavor that truly had value. I pushed past my doubts and now have a thriving online presence.

These powerhouse pointers that Feona offers in her book are meant to not only uplift and motivate you, but also to energize you to accomplish what is already in you. This author is an on-purpose woman of action. I'm excited for you for you're about to reach higher heights.

Blessings to you!

Trevon Sundiata Imhotep Ferguson
Founder/President/CEO House of Jah Inc. & Universal Voice
Author of "The ABC'S of Empowerment"

# Powerhouse Pointer #1

Be careful what you say to and around children. They are taking it all in — good or bad. And, the conversation has lasting effects. You have the power to groom future "world leaders." You want to be a builder not a destroyer. Use your tongue wisely.

# Powerhouse Pointer #2

When you have a "real" friend (I mean one who is ride-or-die, does not judge but offers constructive criticism, stretches and challenges you, has your back emotionally and financially and loves from the heart and not with a hidden agenda), you better hold on to him/her and be a mirror reflection of their friendship. We know many people but not all of them are this type of friend. Cleave to them!

# Powerhouse Pointer #3

It's so easy to get consumed with your own agenda. You want to make major moves, accomplish profound goals, get paid and be famous. But what about making a difference in the life of a young person? To me, this is essential to creating a legacy of service-minded youth that will (with your influence) turn into service-minded adults and community activists. I beg you to identify just one young person today and start to sow into their life. Don't forget that someone did that for you. Right?!

# Powerhouse Pointer #4

Never dumb down what you do to pacify people's insecurities and issues with what they lack. You were designed ON PURPOSE to be magnificent in many areas. Let your light authentically shine through your talents and skill sets so that others will be inspired to follow suit with their respective gifts.

# Powerhouse Pointer #5

Allow your steps to be ordered in humility for it attracts blessings and favor.

# Powerhouse Pointer #6

The Holy Bible tells us that life and death is in the power of the tongue. So what are you saying today? I encourage you to speak positive words. Call goodness into your life. Use your tongue to invite blessings into your world. Remember: What you speak into existence comes back to you.

# Powerhouse Pointer #7

Your mess is your ministry,
and will make you millions.

# Powerhouse Pointer #8

Reading should never be a chore or a bore. You should read for information, inspiration and power. When you read, you expand your mind, travel to places you have yet to go physically, dream dreams that can one day come true, evolve and grow. I dare you to read today for the fun, love and honor it brings. Please incorporate your children into this as well. If they see you doing it, they'll want to do it also, and continue to do so. Reading rocks!

# Powerhouse Pointer #9

A closed mouth does not get fed. So don't be afraid to ask for help today. There's someone out here who will give you what you need if you're bold enough to humbly ask for it.

# Powerhouse Pointer #10

When I wake up in the morning, I'm so excited. That's because I know that my Father has something special for me. And, I'm expecting it. I'm expecting Him to bless me so that I can be a blessing to someone else. I'm expecting Him to expand my territory so that I can do more for my family and community. I'm expecting Him to do more than I could ever imagine for myself.

So, what are you expecting? Expect the best and it will surely come.

# Powerhouse Pointer #11

I remember back in high school, people use to call me "Little Oprah" because I was making power moves in the journalism world. I have long admired Oprah Winfrey. I would tune in to her show everyday at 4 pm with my grandmother to watch her do her thing. She is a true media mogul. But, there is ONLY one Oprah Winfrey. And, there is ONLY one Feona Sharhran Huff. I can't do it like her and she can't do it like me. We are two different people with our own unique personality and skill set. The next time someone calls you the "NEXT" anything, kindly thank them for the association but gently remind them that you are authentic. There's NO ONE like you. You are IT.

# Powerhouse Pointer #12

I have to admit it . . . I love shopping
for dainty sundresses, open-toe heels,
colorful sunglasses and big purses.
However, I will never spend my money
when I know I have a business expense
to pay for or I need to put money aside
for a networking function. So, for all
of you shopping lovers who are also
entrepreneurs, I caution you to put those
clothes back if you catch yourself heading
to the check-out line. You may just need
those funds in case that next business
opportunity comes up.

# Powerhouse Pointer #13

Are you sleeping your talents away?! Wake them up and get busy! Citizens of the world need your gifts in order to move them to their next plateau. We're waiting!

# Powerhouse Pointer #14

In the Holy Bible, the scripture says "you have not because you ask not." You can have an amazing talent, but if you don't ask people to invest in what you have to offer by way of them becoming your client, your talent will go unused and you will stay broke. However, when you put yourself out there and show proof that you can do what you say you can, your asking will yield results beyond your desires. So, position yourself for a power move by asking for what you want.

# Powerhouse Pointer #15

I have noticed so many people are talking about being thankful these days — and not for "things" but for the gift of life. Someone didn't wake up this morning. Someone lost their battle to cancer yesterday. Some are breathing right now but not living life to the fullest. I encourage you to put aside any complaining and lift up your head and hands, and give God some serious praise. Life is great. And, I am thankful!

# Powerhouse Pointer #16

There is a clear difference between cockiness and confidence. I am the latter and will not apologize for it. If someone tries to attack you for being who you are, don't receive it. They have an issue with themselves. You just make sure that you continue to stand firm and stay on your anointed path.

# Powerhouse Pointer #17

One day as I was eating while typing, my bowl of soup fell off of my lap and the juice spilled into my laptop. Although I immediately cleaned up the accident, the damage was done. "Betsy" (my beloved laptop's name!) turned on for a few tries and then she was dead. This wasn't good. I called up the company I purchased her from to find out that I had one-year accidental handling, which covered spills. I am so glad that I put out some extra funds to cover a future accident. I urge you to do the same!

# Powerhouse Pointer #18

I have entered a transitional stage in my life. Initially, it was scary. The unknown is always like that. But once I talked to several members of my support team, I realized that I should embrace this time. This phase is for my good and will be a testimony to the people I later share my experience with. So please, when transition knocks on your door, open it up, let it in and say "Thank You." Your life will be the better because of it.

# Powerhouse Pointer #19

When I wake up in the morning, it's with the spirit of expectancy. I am expecting the favor of God. And, I receive it. I not only want you to anticipate God's favor today, but tomorrow, next week, next year and all throughout your life. When you expect, you will receive.

# Powerhouse Pointer #20

When planning an event, one of your goals may very well be to pack the place. But what happens when you don't get the turnout you desired? Do you cut back on the energy you would have put in the event if it were filled to capacity? NO! The show must go on. You CAN'T control the turnout. You CAN control your delivery. If people don't show, oh well. Your focus should be on the ones who did. They are who really matter.

# Powerhouse Pointer #21

Be ready when you meet people (or reconnect with them). They may have what you need to take your project or cause to the next level or help more people learn about what you do.

# Powerhouse Pointer #22

After crossing the street – bus station bound – I realized that I had forgotten my backpack on wheels. It contained my laptop, lunch and promotional materials. I wanted to go back home, but time didn't permit. I didn't sweat not having my mobile office. I simply focused on other things I could do like make phone calls, check my P.O. Box and scout venue space for upcoming events. I was able to accomplish a lot. Don't stress over anything today. Just go with the flow and watch as you accomplish much.

# Powerhouse Pointer #23

A lot of people will get up this morning dreading the day. To them, it may signify the beginning of a long work experience. They'll totally miss that today is really the start to a beautiful adventure. There's so much to look forward to accomplishing. Embrace the positive possibilities that today (and everyday) brings. You'll certainly get more out of life this way.

# Powerhouse Pointer #24

I get a lot of Facebook "friend" requests. However, before I click "confirm," I screen the potential friend. I want to know what the person is about, the type of activity that they have on their page and the FB company that they keep. I need to see what our commonality is and why they want to be friends. If I don't get the answers I'm searching for, no friendship is formed. The people who share my cyberspace world must be about something. I will not settle. Please be just as mindful with your social media acceptance!

# Powerhouse Pointer #25

Recently, I was watching a tapping of my daughter reciting the poem "Our Deepest Fear" at Kim M. Sudderth's 1st Annual PIP Women into Profit conference. It led me to thinking about how so many people live in fear of fulfilling their destiny. They are afraid of being rejected or ridiculed. They are fearful of the unknown. If this is you and there is something that God has called you to do, I challenge you to push pass that False Evidence Appearing Real (FEAR). You will never win in life from the seat of fear.

# Powerhouse Pointer #26

When you look into the mirror, what do you see? I ask people this very question in my "Mirror Mirror" self-esteem workshop. I believe that what we see determines how we navigate life. If you see a champion when you stand before your reflection, you will be the type to go out and accomplish your goals, desires as well as conquer life's challenges. I dare you to see greatness when you look in the mirror so that you can go out and do great things.

# Powerhouse Pointer #27

Whenever you're on the path to success, you're going to run into what's commonly referred to as "HATERS." These are people who try to get in your way, talk bad about you and look to shoot you down every opportunity they get. I implore you to see them for who they really are: MOTIVATORS! They are the reason you must win.

# Powerhouse Pointer #28

It's a fact of life that you will have disappointments. However, when they come, don't succumb to the feeling of defeat. Start praising God with a mighty faith and assurance that things will work out in His time.

# Powerhouse Pointer #29

You may be feeling a bit frustrated because you haven't achieved your dream as of yet. However, you must not allow your dream to die. You are so close to claiming it. I can feel it for you. Your job is to keep pressing on. Do something every day toward your desire. If you really want it, you won't quit. Besides, giving up is not in your DNA. I have faith in you. Have faith in yourself and know that God will give you the desires of your heart.

# Powerhouse Pointer #30

Let your work ethic be diligent and action-based as well as result producing. Your next client could be waiting in the wings and watching you work.

# Powerhouse Pointer #31

I was feeling a bit down one A.M. In
trying to work through my emotions,
I stopped by a women's clothing store
where my friend is the manager. Tisha
and I talked about staying the course in
the midst of challenges; to be steadfast
no matter what. By the conclusion of our
conversation, I was back to the powerful
thinking woman that I know and love.
Don't let your emotions rule your day. Talk
it out with people who love you.

# Powerhouse Pointer #32

Value your time today by disregarding anyone who calls or stops you to gossip, shoot the breeze or have conversation that doesn't mirror your action plan. Once time is gone, you can't get it back. Maximize on your seconds, minutes and hours so you can spend your time on important matters.

# Powerhouse Pointer #33

When spring time sets in you indulge in the "Spring Cleaning" ritual. You throw out old clothes, furniture, papers and such. You refuse to go into the next season with old stuff. You want better for your space. Please do this with the people in your life as well. Some don't belong in your space anymore. You need to move forward and some folks just aren't meant to come along any longer.

# Powerhouse Pointer #34

Don't let your dream dwindle or die just because people are not supporting you in droves. God planted the seed for your dream within you for YOU to manifest. He has given you the heart, tenacity and skill set to see it bloom. Believe in yourself and work on your dream everyday. I can't wait for your praise report. I will surely share mine.

# Powerhouse Pointer #35

Do you know how to let go of a toxic relationship, friendship, working environment or anything else that causes you emotional, mental, spiritual or physical harm? If not, here's some simple but savvy advice that I personally adhere to . . . LET GO! The longer you hold on, the longer you're going to suffer, get sick, cry your eyes out, develop ulcers, lose your hair, go gray, age poorly, etc. Your life is precious. Those who you let in as well as the things you do and the work you engage in should mirror you. Take a stand, say "NO MORE" and let the door usher drama, pain and heartache goodbye. Now go on and live your life in peace.

# Powerhouse Pointer #36

Bartering is a basic principle founded many years ago that still holds value today. The key to exchanging a service for a service is that all parties involved equally benefit. The way the economy is now, we should be open to barter with each other. And, in the end, everybody wins.

# Powerhouse Pointer #37

If you ever feel mistreated while shopping, please exercise your right to report your issue to the powers that be. The store employee can't get away with anything if you let your voice be heard through the good ol' pen, an email to the corporate office and a phone call to the complaint center. These methods will accomplish your mission for justice.

# Powerhouse Pointer #38

If you are an employer and have to lay someone off, do so with decency and professionalism. Don't mail off a termination letter when you can call your employee in for a face-to-face exit interview. Just as there is karma with how you treat people on a personal level, so it is in the professional arena. What goes around comes back around.

# Powerhouse Pointer #39

You can't become a powerful person from the seat of your comfort zone. Dare to step into your greatness right now. You will then be able to conquer higher heights, accomplish bigger goals, move mighty mountains and be a shining example of a relentless powerhouse.

# Powerhouse Pointer #40

Don't you know that you are so abundantly blessed right now?! You woke up. Blessed. You are able to connect with people around the world with the click of the mouse. Blessed. You are eating dinner whereas someone else is going hungry. Blessed. You have clothes to wear. Blessed. You are fully literate and able to read this message. Blessed.

# Powerhouse Pointer #41

A closed fist doesn't profit you. With clinched fingers, you can't give or receive blessings. Open up your hands and the universe will open up to you.

# Powerhouse Pointer #42

These days, many people are heavily immersed in the ways of social media and technology. You'll get an email or website in box message before you receive a phone call and a text will pop up on your cell phone rather than your mobile ringing for a live conversation. The problem with this is that "human connection" is compromised. Voice to voice and face to face interaction become a thing of the past. It's not too late, though. The "old school" way is still powerful. Try it. Call someone up. Invite your friend to lunch. Laugh in person. You will feel alive and connected far stronger than any technology tool can offer.

# Powerhouse Pointer #43

Looking into the mirror is more than just about ensuring that your wardrobe is in tact, your hair is flawless, your makeup is just right or your teeth are sans broccoli. On a deeper level, it's to see yourself for who you truly are: An empowered person with powerful gifts to contribute to the world. You must see this for yourself when you look at you. So, see the beauty of your existence then walk in your divine assignment. This will encourage others to do the same.

# Powerhouse Pointer #44

You are valuable. And, your work has value. So, when people try to take advantage of you or undermine your worth or skill set, politely pronounce that you've got it going on and either urge them to exit "stage right" or think "deuces" and get moving so that your time isn't wasted, your energy isn't drained and your talent isn't compromised.

# Powerhouse Pointer #45

It's very easy to hold a grudge against people for doing you wrong. You may think you hold the power in not forgiving them. But, you don't—they do. You must forgive so that you can be free. Besides, what if someone continued to be mad at you? Would you like that?

# Powerhouse Pointer #46

When you're working for a purpose and not seeking self-praise, the results will be rewarding and all will most certainly benefit!

# Powerhouse Pointer #47

Stop comparing yourself to other people. You don't know what it took for them to get where they are and if you found out, who knows if you'd be willing to go through what they had to endure. Focus your attention on the steps you're taking to reach your success and make sure you are doing so in decency and order.

# Powerhouse Pointer #48

You are sure to experience tight financial times at some point in this lifetime. So, when money is low or not there, you must get creative and thrifty. Barter with someone. Clip out coupons. Rent a movie instead of going to the theater. Fix dinner at home. When done with a positive spirit, you will have fun making ends meet and the focus on dollars and cents won't rock your world.

# Powerhouse Pointer #49

If you desire to go into business for yourself, I encourage you to do it. Will you be criticized? Probably so. Will those who you thought would support you make excuses as to why they now can't? Probably so. Will you struggle as you strive to get your venture off the ground? Probably so. But, so what?! You'll never know the success you can have and the lives you can touch through your entrepreneurial endeavor if you don't give it a try. As long as you believe in yourself and are diligent in seeing your efforts through, you have a fighting chance.

# Powerhouse Pointer #50

You have a story to tell, a testimony to share and people to help heal. One of the greatest ways to do this is by writing a book. And, there is a book project inside of you. It doesn't matter how many pages it is, the content is what's imperative. Take some time after reading this final Powerhouse Pointer to consider what subject matter you'd like to write about. Make sure to grab a pen and notepad to jot down your thoughts. It will come together and the next thing you know, I'll be reading your book.